Boosting productivity involves improving focus, efficiency, and output in a sustainable way. Here are some strategies to help enhance productivity:

1. Time Management

- Prioritize tasks: Use the Eisenhower Matrix (urgent vs. important) to decide what needs attention first.
- Time blocking: Dedicate specific times to different tasks to avoid distractions.
- Pomodoro technique: Work in short, focused intervals (e.g., 25 minutes), followed by a 5-minute break.

2. Task Management

- To-do lists: Break down tasks into manageable chunks and track progress.
- Delegation: Don't hesitate to delegate tasks that others can handle, allowing you to focus on high-priority work.
- Automation: Use software tools to automate repetitive tasks, such as scheduling, reminders, or data entry.

3. Eliminate Distractions

- Create a dedicated workspace: Minimize interruptions by having a quiet, organized area for work.
- Turn off notifications: Disable non-urgent notifications to reduce distractions.
- Set boundaries: Inform others of your focused work periods to minimize disturbances.

4. Improve Focus

- Mindfulness and meditation: Practices like deep breathing or meditation help improve focus and mental clarity.
- Task batching: Group similar tasks together to avoid switching between different types of activities.

5. Health and Well-being

- Regular exercise: Physical activity improves mental clarity and overall energy levels.
- Proper sleep: Ensure adequate sleep to recharge and maintain cognitive performance.
- Healthy diet: Eating well can boost brain function and prevent energy crashes.

6. Leverage Technology

- Productivity tools: Tools like Trello, Asana, or Notion can help you organize and track your tasks.
- Focus apps: Apps like Forest, Focus@Will, or RescueTime can help limit distractions and track your productivity.

7. Continuous Learning

- Skill development: Regularly update and improve your skills to increase your efficiency and adaptability.
- Feedback loops: Seek feedback from colleagues or mentors to identify areas for improvement.

By combining these approaches, you can steadily improve your productivity over time. Start with a few strategies and build upon them as you find what works best for you!

Effective time management is crucial for increasing productivity, reducing stress, and achieving your goals. Here are some time management techniques and tips to help you stay organized and make the most of your time:

1. Prioritize Tasks

- Eisenhower Matrix: Categorize tasks into four quadrants:
    - Urgent and Important: Do these tasks immediately.

- Important, but Not Urgent: Schedule these tasks.
- Urgent, but Not Important: Delegate these tasks if possible.
- Neither Urgent nor Important: Consider eliminating these tasks.
- ABCDE Method: Assign each task a letter (A = Most important, E = Least important) to help you prioritize what to focus on first.

2. Time Blocking

- Allocate specific blocks of time to work on specific tasks or projects. For example, dedicate 9:00 AM – 11:00 AM to deep work, 11:00 AM – 12:00 PM to meetings, and 1:00 PM – 3:00 PM to creative work. This helps avoid multitasking and distractions.
- Set breaks: Don't forget to schedule short breaks to recharge.

3. Pomodoro Technique

- Work in focused intervals, typically 25 minutes, followed by a 5-minute break. After four intervals, take a longer break (15-30 minutes). This technique helps maintain focus and prevents burnout.

4. The 2-Minute Rule

- If a task will take less than 2 minutes to complete, do it immediately. This prevents small tasks from piling up and helps maintain momentum throughout the day.

5. Set SMART Goals

- Specific: Be clear about what you want to achieve.
- Measurable: Ensure there is a way to track progress.
- Achievable: Set realistic goals.
- Relevant: Ensure goals align with your broader objectives.
- Time-bound: Define a deadline for completion.

6. Batch Similar Tasks

- Group similar tasks together to save time. For example, check and respond to emails at specific times during the day, rather than throughout the day. This minimizes task switching and boosts efficiency.

7. Use Technology

- Task Management Tools: Use apps like Trello, Todoist, or Asana to organize and track your tasks.
- Calendar apps: Use digital calendars to schedule time blocks, meetings, and reminders.
- Time Tracking Apps: Apps like RescueTime, Toggl, or Clockify help track how you're spending your time and identify areas for improvement.

8. Limit Distractions

- Turn off notifications: Disable non-urgent notifications on your phone or computer.
- Use the "Do Not Disturb" mode: Set your devices to "Do Not Disturb" to maintain focus.
- Create a focused work environment: Organize your workspace to be free from distractions and clutter.

9. Delegate and Outsource

- If you have tasks that others can do, delegate them to free up your time for higher-priority work.

10. Review and Reflect

- At the end of each day or week, reflect on what you accomplished and what needs improvement. Adjust your time management strategy accordingly for better results in the future.

By using these time management strategies consistently, you can achieve more in less time, reduce stress, and maintain a better work-life balance.

Task management is about organizing, prioritizing, and completing tasks efficiently to achieve your goals. It involves setting clear objectives, breaking tasks into manageable steps, and using tools or methods to track progress. Here are strategies and techniques for effective task management:

1. **Set Clear Goals**

- Define the end goal: Understand the overall objective for each project or task.
- Break it down: Split larger tasks into smaller, more manageable parts. This makes them less overwhelming and easier to track.
- Set deadlines: Assign deadlines to each task or subtask to ensure progress is made and goals are met on time.

2. **Prioritize Tasks**

- Eisenhower Matrix: Categorize tasks as:
    - Urgent and Important: Do these first.
    - Important, but Not Urgent: Schedule these tasks.
    - Urgent, but Not Important: Delegate these if possible.
    - Neither Urgent nor Important: Consider eliminating these tasks.
- ABC Method: Label tasks as A (most important), B (important but not critical), or C (low-priority) to help you focus on high-value activities.

3. **Task Lists**

- Daily To-Do List: Create a list of tasks to accomplish each day. Keep it realistic and manageable.
- Master List: Keep a master list of all your tasks, categorized by project or priority. Review and update it regularly.
- Use Task Management Tools: Tools like Trello, Asana, Todoist, or Notion help you organize, categorize, and track tasks in a visually clear way.

4. Time Allocation

- Time Blocking: Set aside dedicated blocks of time for different tasks or projects to stay focused and prevent multitasking.
- The 2-Minute Rule: If a task takes less than 2 minutes to complete, do it immediately to avoid putting it off.
- Pomodoro Technique: Use 25-minute work intervals with short breaks to stay focused and productive.

5. Delegate Tasks

- Identify tasks for delegation: Recognize tasks that others can handle to free up time for higher-priority work.
- Assign clearly: When delegating, communicate expectations, deadlines, and any necessary resources clearly.

6. Track Progress

- Monitor your progress: Regularly check the status of tasks and projects to ensure you're on track.
- Adjust as needed: If something isn't working, adjust your strategy, either by shifting priorities or modifying deadlines.

7. Avoid Procrastination

- Start with the hardest task: Tackle the most challenging task first (also known as "eating the frog"), as this sets a productive tone for the day.

- Set small goals: Breaking tasks into smaller steps can make them feel more achievable and reduce procrastination.

8. Review and Reflect

- End-of-day review: At the end of each day, evaluate what you accomplished and what still needs attention.
- Weekly reflection: Assess your progress over the week and adjust your task list for the upcoming week.

9. Limit Multitasking

- Focus on one task at a time: Studies show multitasking reduces efficiency and quality of work. Focusing on one task until completion will improve productivity.

10. Celebrate Small Wins

- Reward yourself: Celebrate completing tasks or reaching milestones, even if small, to stay motivated.

By applying these task management techniques, you can stay organized, focus on what's important, and improve your ability to achieve goals effectively. The key is to find a system that works for you and stick with it consistently.

Eliminating distractions is a crucial step in improving focus, productivity, and overall efficiency. Distractions can derail your progress and waste time, so it's essential to create an environment and routine that minimizes interruptions. Here are strategies to help eliminate distractions:

1. Create a Dedicated Workspace

- Designate a specific area for work: Whether it's a home office or a specific corner of a room, having a designated workspace helps signal to your brain that it's time to focus.
- Minimize clutter: Keep your workspace clean and organized. Clutter can create visual distractions and add to stress.

2. Turn Off Notifications

- Disable phone notifications: Turn off non-essential app alerts or set your phone to "Do Not Disturb" during focused work periods.
- Mute email alerts: Constant email notifications can disrupt your workflow. Check emails at set intervals, rather than immediately when they come in.

3. Use Technology to Block Distractions

- Website blockers: Use apps like Freedom, Cold Turkey, or StayFocusd to block distracting websites or social media during work hours.
- Focus apps: Use apps like Forest, Focus@Will, or Pomodone to help you stay on track by promoting focus through timers and productivity tracking.
- Set timers: Use the Pomodoro technique or set a timer for focused work periods (e.g., 25 minutes) with breaks in between.

4. Set Boundaries with Others

- Communicate with family or colleagues: If you work from home or in an open office, let others know your focused work hours and ask for minimal interruptions.
- Create signals: Use a "do not disturb" sign or a simple visual signal to let others know when you're in deep work mode.
- Set up meeting-free times: Block out specific times in your calendar for focused work where meetings are avoided.

5. Limit Digital Distractions

- Organize your devices: Keep only the apps and documents you need for your current task visible and closed other distractions.
- Declutter your desktop: Having too many files or open applications on your computer screen can be overwhelming and distracting.

6. Optimize Your Environment

- Control background noise: Use noise-cancelling headphones or listen to background music that helps you concentrate (e.g., instrumental or binaural beats).
- Use ambient lighting: Poor lighting can strain your eyes and reduce focus. Opt for natural light or a well-lit workspace.
- Comfortable seating: Ensure your chair and desk setup is comfortable, so you're not distracted by discomfort.

7. Practice Single-Tasking

- Avoid multitasking: Studies show that multitasking can actually reduce productivity. Focus on one task at a time to improve concentration and efficiency.
- Prioritize: Stick to the most important tasks first and avoid switching between tasks too frequently.

8. Time Management and Scheduling

- Set time limits for tasks: Give yourself a specific time frame to work on tasks and take regular breaks.
- Time blocking: Assign specific time blocks for focused work, ensuring there's a clear start and end time to each activity.
- Plan ahead: Prepare a daily or weekly schedule to reduce the likelihood of being pulled into non-essential tasks.

9. Mindset and Mental Focus

- Practice mindfulness: Mindfulness techniques like deep breathing can help center your focus and reduce mental distractions.
- Stay organized: Use task lists, planners, or productivity tools to keep track of your to-do items, reducing the need to multitask or worry about forgetting tasks.

10. Take Breaks

- Prevent burnout: Taking regular breaks helps refresh your mind and body, improving your ability to stay focused when you return to work.
- Follow the Pomodoro technique: After each 25-minute work session, take a 5-minute break to recharge, and after four sessions, take a longer break (15-30 minutes).

11. Reduce Environmental Triggers

- Silence your phone: If you don't need your phone for work, put it in another room or out of sight to avoid the temptation to check it.
- Organize your digital files: Keep your computer desktop and file system organized to reduce distractions from searching for documents.

By eliminating distractions and adopting a focused, deliberate approach to your work, you can significantly increase your productivity and stay on track toward achieving your goals.

Improving focus is key to enhancing productivity, managing tasks efficiently, and achieving your goals. Here are practical strategies to help you boost and maintain your focus throughout the day:

1. Set Clear Goals

- **Break down tasks:** Make sure your goals are clear and broken down into smaller, manageable chunks. This helps prevent feeling overwhelmed and keeps you focused on one step at a time.
- **SMART goals:** Ensure your goals are Specific, Measurable, Achievable, Relevant, and Time-bound.

2. Use the Pomodoro Technique

- **Work in intervals:** Use focused work periods of 25 minutes, followed by a 5-minute break. After four intervals, take a longer break (15-30 minutes). This method helps prevent burnout and maintains mental clarity.
- **Set a timer:** Having a set time for work helps train your brain to focus for short bursts and relax during breaks.

3. Limit Distractions

- **Turn off notifications:** Disable notifications from social media, email, and apps to avoid interruptions while working.
- **Create a distraction-free workspace:** Set up a workspace with minimal distractions, including a clean desk and a quiet environment.
- **Use website blockers:** Tools like Cold Turkey, Freedom, or StayFocusd can block distracting websites while you work.

4. Time Blocking

- **Schedule specific tasks:** Set aside time blocks for focused work on specific tasks or projects. Make sure to avoid multitasking during these blocks.
- **Set boundaries for meetings and tasks:** Protect your work time by setting boundaries around meetings, social media, and other time sinks.

5. Practice Mindfulness

- Mindful breathing exercises: Take a few minutes to practice deep breathing or mindfulness before diving into work. This can help clear your mind and reduce stress, enhancing your focus.
- Meditation: Short daily meditation sessions (5-10 minutes) can improve attention, reduce anxiety, and increase focus over time.
- Focus on the present: Remind yourself to be present and engaged in whatever task you're working on. Avoid the temptation to jump to the next task prematurely.

6. Exercise Regularly

- Physical activity boosts mental clarity: Regular exercise increases blood flow to the brain, improves mood, and reduces stress, all of which help you stay focused.
- Short walks: Take a brisk walk during breaks to reset your mind and body.

7. Maintain Proper Sleep

- Get quality sleep: Aim for 7-9 hours of sleep each night. Poor sleep affects cognitive function, attention, and focus.
- Create a bedtime routine: Set a consistent sleep schedule and avoid screens before bed to ensure restful sleep.

8. Stay Hydrated and Eat Well

- Drink water: Dehydration can impair concentration, so make sure to drink enough water throughout the day.
- Eat brain-boosting foods: Incorporate foods rich in antioxidants, healthy fats, and proteins (e.g., berries, nuts, leafy greens, and fish) to support cognitive function.

9. Use Focused Work Music or Sounds

- Background music: Some people find that instrumental music or sounds like white noise, nature sounds, or binaural beats help them concentrate. Experiment to find what works best for you.

- Noise-canceling headphones: If you're in a noisy environment, use noise-canceling headphones to block out distractions.

10. Take Regular Breaks

- Avoid burnout: Regular breaks are essential to maintaining focus. Short breaks (5-10 minutes) after periods of focused work allow your brain to rest and reset.
- Stretch or move: Use breaks to stretch, walk around, or perform a light physical activity to rejuvenate your mind and body.

11. Practice Single-Tasking

- Focus on one task at a time: Multitasking can divide your attention and reduce the quality of your work. Instead, focus on completing one task before moving on to the next.
- Task batching: Group similar tasks together to reduce the cognitive load and maintain focus on one category of work.

12. Declutter Your Workspace

- Keep it organized: A cluttered workspace can cause mental clutter, making it harder to focus. Keep only the essentials within reach, and regularly tidy your desk or workspace.
- Clear digital distractions: Keep your computer desktop organized and close only the apps or documents you need.

13. Motivate Yourself with Rewards

- Reward yourself: After completing a task or reaching a milestone, treat yourself to something small as a reward (e.g., a snack, a short break, or a relaxing activity).
- Visual progress trackers: Use a visual tool, such as a checklist or progress bar, to track your accomplishments and stay motivated.

14. Reduce Mental Fatigue

- Change up tasks: Switch between different types of tasks (e.g., creative work, administrative work) to avoid mental fatigue from doing the same thing for too long.
- Take power naps: Short naps (10-20 minutes) can recharge your focus without making you groggy.

By incorporating these strategies, you can significantly improve your focus and enhance your ability to work efficiently. The key is to experiment with different approaches and find what helps you stay engaged and productive.

Improving focus involves creating an environment and mindset that supports sustained concentration and reduces distractions. Here are some additional techniques to help you boost your focus:

1. Set Clear and Specific Goals

- Define your objectives: Make sure you know exactly what you need to accomplish, whether it's a daily task or a long-term project.
- Break down large tasks: Divide complex tasks into smaller, manageable steps so that you're not overwhelmed and can maintain focus on one thing at a time.
- Use the "two-minute rule": If a task can be done in two minutes or less, do it immediately, rather than letting it linger and clutter your mind.

2. Use Time Management Techniques

- Pomodoro Technique: Work in blocks of time (usually 25 minutes) followed by short breaks (5 minutes). After four cycles, take a longer break (15-30 minutes).
- Time Blocking: Dedicate specific chunks of time for different tasks, and make sure to only work on one task during that period. This can improve your ability to concentrate fully on one thing.
- Set deadlines: Even for tasks that aren't time-sensitive, having a deadline can create a sense of urgency and help you stay on track.

3. Limit Distractions

- Turn off notifications: Disable non-essential notifications on your phone and computer to reduce interruptions.
- Use website blockers: Use tools like Freedom, StayFocusd, or Cold Turkey to block distracting websites during work hours.
- Work offline: If possible, disconnect from the internet or use apps that block internet access while working.

4. Optimize Your Environment

- Minimize clutter: Keep your workspace organized to avoid distractions and create a visually clean environment that signals focus.
- Design a quiet space: If you're in a noisy environment, consider using noise-cancelling headphones or listening to instrumental music, white noise, or binaural beats that can enhance focus.
- Comfortable setup: Ensure your desk, chair, and computer setup are ergonomically comfortable to avoid physical discomfort that could lead to distractions.

5. Take Regular Breaks

- Avoid burnout: Regular breaks help refresh your mind and improve focus. Use techniques like the Pomodoro method or take a break every 90 minutes to ensure you don't become mentally fatigued.
- Physical movement: Stretch or walk around during breaks to increase circulation and relieve tension.

6. Prioritize Sleep and Rest

- Get enough sleep: Aim for 7-9 hours of quality sleep per night, as sleep deprivation negatively affects concentration and memory.
- Create a sleep routine: Go to bed at the same time each night and avoid screen time right before bed to improve sleep quality.

- Napping: A short nap (10-20 minutes) can rejuvenate your focus and energy levels during the day.

7. Practice Mindfulness

- Mindfulness exercises: Techniques like deep breathing, meditation, and progressive muscle relaxation help train your brain to stay present and focused.
- Mindful pauses: Take a moment before starting a task to center yourself and focus on the present moment, reducing the likelihood of distractions.

8. Use Focus-Boosting Tools

- Focus apps: Apps like Forest or Focus@Will offer tools to keep you focused. Forest, for instance, helps you stay off your phone by growing a virtual tree as long as you stay focused.
- Productivity apps: Use task management apps like Todoist, Trello, or Notion to organize your tasks and maintain a clear structure for your day.
- White noise: Use apps like Noisli to play background sounds like rain or nature that can help you stay focused without being distracted by your environment.

9. Fuel Your Brain

- Hydration: Dehydration can impair focus, so ensure you drink plenty of water throughout the day.
- Brain foods: Foods rich in omega-3 fatty acids (like fish), antioxidants (like berries), and complex carbs (like whole grains) help improve cognitive function.
- Avoid heavy meals: Eating large or sugary meals can cause sluggishness and reduce concentration. Opt for lighter, balanced meals.

10. Stay Organized

- Declutter your mind: Use task management systems to get your ideas out of your head and into a trusted system, reducing mental clutter.

- Create a daily plan: Outline what you need to accomplish each day, setting priorities and creating a clear agenda.
- Review and adjust: At the end of the day or week, reflect on your progress and adjust your goals, strategies, and environment as needed.

11. Adopt a Growth Mindset

- Embrace challenges: Instead of avoiding tasks that feel difficult, approach them as opportunities for growth. A positive mindset increases resilience and helps you push through focus challenges.
- Celebrate progress: Recognize and celebrate small wins throughout the day to maintain motivation and reinforce your ability to stay focused.

12. Exercise Regularly

- Boost mental clarity: Physical exercise increases blood flow to the brain, which can enhance focus and cognitive performance.
- Quick exercise sessions: Even short bursts of physical activity—like a 5-minute walk or stretch—can improve mental clarity and focus.

13. Avoid Multitasking

- Focus on one task: Multitasking divides your attention and reduces efficiency. Prioritize single-tasking to improve the quality of your work and sustain your focus for longer periods.
- Batch tasks: Group similar tasks together to minimize the switching of gears and maintain sustained attention on related activities.

By combining these strategies, you can create an environment and mindset conducive to improved focus, helping you become more productive and achieve your goals efficiently.

Health and well-being are essential components of a balanced and fulfilling life. Taking care of both physical and mental health can improve your productivity, focus, relationships, and overall happiness. Here are key areas to focus on for improving health and well-being:

1. Physical Health

- Exercise Regularly: Aim for at least 30 minutes of moderate exercise most days of the week. Activities like walking, running, swimming, or strength training help improve cardiovascular health, increase energy, and reduce stress.
    - Benefits: Improves heart health, increases energy, boosts mood, supports weight management, strengthens muscles and bones.
- Sleep Well: Prioritize sleep by aiming for 7-9 hours each night. Poor sleep can impair cognitive function, memory, and physical health.
    - Tips for Better Sleep:
        - Set a regular sleep schedule.
        - Avoid caffeine and electronics at least 30 minutes before bed.
        - Create a calming bedtime routine (e.g., reading, relaxing music).
- Eat a Balanced Diet: Include a variety of fruits, vegetables, whole grains, healthy fats, and lean proteins in your meals.
    - Tips for Healthy Eating:
        - Avoid highly processed foods, sugars, and excessive fats.
        - Stay hydrated by drinking plenty of water.
        - Plan meals ahead of time to ensure balanced nutrition.
- Preventive Care: Regular check-ups, screenings, and vaccinations can help identify health issues early and prevent serious problems.

2. Mental and Emotional Well-being

- Stress Management: Learn to manage stress through relaxation techniques like deep breathing, meditation, or progressive muscle relaxation.
    - Tips for Managing Stress:
        - Practice mindfulness or meditation daily.
        - Engage in hobbies or activities you enjoy to relax.
        - Set realistic goals and break tasks into manageable steps.

- **Positive Thinking:** Cultivate a positive mindset by practicing gratitude, affirmations, and focusing on the present.
  - How to Stay Positive:
    - Keep a gratitude journal, noting things you're thankful for each day.
    - Reframe negative thoughts into positive ones.
    - Surround yourself with positive influences and uplifting environments.
- **Seek Support:** Don't hesitate to talk to someone about your feelings. Social connections are vital for emotional health.
  - Ways to Build Social Support:
    - Maintain strong relationships with family and friends.
    - Join social or interest-based groups to meet new people.
    - Seek professional help (e.g., therapist, counselor) when needed.

3. Mental Stimulation and Cognitive Health

- **Engage in Lifelong Learning:** Keep your brain active by learning new skills, reading, or solving puzzles.
  - How to Stimulate Your Mind:
    - Read books, articles, or take online courses on topics that interest you.
    - Play games like chess, puzzles, or strategy games to improve cognitive function.
    - Practice a new language or musical instrument.
- **Practice Mindfulness and Meditation:** Mindfulness exercises, such as meditation or breathing exercises, help improve focus, reduce anxiety, and increase self-awareness.
  - How to Practice Mindfulness:
    - Set aside time each day for deep breathing or guided meditation.
    - Practice being present in the moment, focusing on what's happening now, instead of worrying about the past or future.

4. Work-Life Balance

- Set Boundaries: Learn to say no when needed and set clear boundaries between work and personal life. Work-life balance is crucial to mental and emotional well-being.
    - Tips for Balance:
        - Set working hours and unplug after work.
        - Take regular breaks during work to recharge.
        - Engage in leisure activities and hobbies to unwind.
- Prioritize Self-Care: Make time for activities that nourish your body and soul, such as taking a walk, having a relaxing bath, or enjoying a hobby.
    - Ideas for Self-Care:
        - Take time for activities you love, like reading, art, or spending time in nature.
        - Schedule regular "me time" to recharge mentally and physically.

5. Self-Compassion and Personal Growth

- Practice Self-Love: Be kind and compassionate toward yourself. Don't be too hard on yourself when you make mistakes, and embrace your imperfections.
    - How to Show Self-Compassion:
        - Speak to yourself with kindness, as you would to a friend.
        - Acknowledge your achievements and progress.
        - Set realistic expectations and be patient with yourself.
- Personal Growth: Focus on continuous improvement in all aspects of life, whether it's personal, professional, or spiritual growth.
    - Ways to Grow:
        - Set personal development goals (e.g., learn a new skill, work on communication).
        - Step outside your comfort zone to try new experiences.
        - Reflect on your progress and adjust your goals accordingly.

6. Building Resilience

- Adapt to Change: Resilience is the ability to adapt to challenges and setbacks. Build your resilience by learning coping strategies and staying flexible in tough situations.
    - Ways to Build Resilience:

- Focus on what you can control in difficult situations.
- Learn from failures and see them as opportunities for growth.
- Reach out for support when facing adversity.
- Cultivate Emotional Intelligence: Emotional intelligence (EQ) is the ability to understand and manage your emotions and those of others. Building EQ can improve relationships and mental health.
    - Ways to Improve EQ:
        - Practice self-awareness by regularly checking in with your emotions.
        - Develop empathy by actively listening to others.
        - Manage emotions by practicing techniques like mindfulness and positive self-talk.

7. Spiritual Well-being (Optional for Some)

- Find Meaning and Purpose: Explore your beliefs and values to create a sense of purpose. For some, spiritual practices, religion, or personal philosophy are important for well-being.
    - How to Find Purpose:
        - Reflect on what brings you joy and fulfillment.
        - Volunteer or engage in acts of kindness to create a positive impact on others.
        - Practice mindfulness, prayer, or spiritual reflection, depending on your belief system.

8. Environmental Health

- Create a Positive Environment: Surround yourself with a supportive environment that promotes your well-being. Whether at home or work, make sure your space is clean, organized, and calming.
    - How to Optimize Your Environment:
        - Decorate with plants, soothing colors, or personal items that bring you comfort.
        - Keep your environment tidy and clutter-free.
        - Use natural light and good airflow to create a refreshing atmosphere.

By focusing on these areas of health and well-being, you can improve both your physical and mental state, leading to a happier, more fulfilling life. It's important to recognize that well-being is an ongoing journey, and small, consistent actions can lead to big improvements over time.

Leveraging technology can significantly improve various aspects of life, from productivity to health management and communication. By utilizing the right tools and platforms, you can enhance efficiency, streamline tasks, and stay connected. Here's how you can leverage technology to improve different areas of your life:

1. Productivity and Task Management

- Task Management Apps: Use apps like Trello, Asana, or Todoist to organize and track tasks. These platforms allow you to break down projects into manageable tasks, set deadlines, and track progress in real time.
- Time Management Tools: Use tools like Toggl or RescueTime to track how you spend your time. This helps identify time-wasters and improve focus.
- Automated Scheduling: Tools like Calendly allow others to book time with you based on your availability, eliminating back-and-forth emails. Similarly, tools like Google Calendar help you manage and set reminders for appointments, meetings, and personal activities.
- Focus Tools: Use apps like Forest or Focus@Will to maintain focus during work. Forest helps you stay off your phone by growing a virtual tree, and Focus@Will offers scientifically designed music to improve concentration.

2. Health and Fitness Tracking

- Fitness Trackers: Devices like the Fitbit, Apple Watch, or Oura Ring track your physical activity, monitor sleep quality, and even provide insights into your heart rate and other health metrics.
- Health Apps: Use apps like MyFitnessPal to track your diet and calorie intake or Headspace and Calm for guided meditation and stress management.

- Exercise Programs: Platforms like Peloton, Nike Training Club, or Aaptiv provide structured workout plans, from cycling and running to yoga and strength training, allowing you to exercise at home or on the go.
- Sleep Trackers: Apps like Sleep Cycle or Pillow monitor your sleep patterns and help you optimize sleep by providing recommendations for improving your sleep quality.

3. Mental Well-being

- Meditation and Mindfulness: Use apps like Headspace, Calm, or Insight Timer to practice mindfulness, reduce stress, and improve emotional well-being. Many of these apps also offer guided meditation sessions tailored to specific needs, like anxiety relief or sleep improvement.
- Therapy and Counseling: Teletherapy platforms like BetterHelp and Talkspace provide access to licensed therapists and counselors from the comfort of your home.
- Mood Tracking: Apps like Moodpath or Daylio let you track your mood, identify patterns, and reflect on your emotional health over time.
- Journaling Apps: Digital journals like Penzu or Day One allow you to reflect on your thoughts and emotions, helping to manage mental health and boost self-awareness.

4. Learning and Personal Growth

- Online Courses: Platforms like Coursera, Udemy, and LinkedIn Learning provide a vast array of courses on various topics, from professional development to personal interests.
- Skill-Building Apps: Apps like Duolingo (for languages), Skillshare (for creative skills), or Khan Academy (for academic subjects) help you learn new skills at your own pace.
- E-books and Audiobooks: Use platforms like Audible for audiobooks or Kindle for e-books to read or listen to books on the go, helping you learn and grow in a flexible manner.
- Flashcards: Use apps like Anki or Quizlet to create and review digital flashcards for learning new concepts, from languages to professional certifications.

5. Financial Management

- Budgeting and Expense Tracking: Use apps like Mint, YNAB (You Need A Budget), or PocketGuard to track your expenses, set savings goals, and stick to a budget.
- Investment Platforms: Platforms like Robinhood, Acorns, and E*TRADE allow you to manage your investments, whether it's in stocks, mutual funds, or retirement savings, often with low fees and easy-to-use interfaces.
- Bill Payment and Automation: Services like Truebill or Prism help automate bill payments and track upcoming payments, reducing the risk of missed bills and late fees.
- Cryptocurrency Management: Platforms like Coinbase or Binance allow you to buy, sell, and track cryptocurrency investments easily from your phone or computer.

6. Social Connectivity and Communication

- Video Calling: Platforms like Zoom, Google Meet, or Microsoft Teams allow you to stay connected with colleagues, friends, and family, especially when remote work or travel is involved.
- Social Media: Tools like Hootsuite or Buffer allow you to manage multiple social media accounts, schedule posts, and track engagement, making it easier to maintain an online presence without constant manual effort.
- Messaging Platforms: Apps like WhatsApp, Slack, or Telegram help you stay in touch with friends, family, or coworkers in real-time, supporting text, voice, and video communication.
- Digital Collaboration: Tools like Google Drive, Dropbox, or OneDrive allow for cloud storage and collaboration on documents, spreadsheets, and presentations, making teamwork more efficient.

7. Home Automation and Smart Devices

- Smart Home Devices: Use devices like Amazon Alexa, Google Nest, or Apple HomeKit to control lighting, heating, and even appliances with voice commands, improving convenience and comfort at home.

- Smart Plugs and Thermostats: Devices like Nest Thermostat or Wemo Smart Plugs allow you to manage your home's energy consumption, helping you save money and live more sustainably.
- Security: Smart security cameras, like those from Ring or Arlo, provide remote monitoring of your home, increasing peace of mind.

8. Entertainment and Relaxation

- Streaming Services: Platforms like Netflix, Hulu, Disney+, and Spotify allow you to access movies, TV shows, music, and podcasts on-demand, providing entertainment tailored to your preferences.
- Gaming: Use gaming consoles or mobile apps like PlayStation, Xbox, or Steam to engage in interactive entertainment and connect with others in gaming communities.
- E-books and Audiobooks: Use Audible or Kindle for portable and accessible reading or listening to books for leisure and personal growth.
- Virtual Reality (VR): VR platforms like Oculus or HTC Vive provide immersive experiences for gaming, education, and relaxation.

9. Environmental Impact

- Energy Monitoring: Use smart meters or apps like Sense to monitor and reduce your home's energy consumption, helping lower your carbon footprint.
- Sustainable Shopping: Apps like Good On You or Buycott allow you to make more sustainable purchasing decisions by providing information about brands' environmental and ethical practices.
- Carbon Footprint Tracking: Use tools like Earth Hero or Joro to track and reduce your carbon footprint by adjusting your lifestyle choices.

10. Virtual Collaboration

- Team Collaboration Tools: Platforms like Slack, Notion, and Monday.com provide digital workspaces for teams to collaborate, share files, communicate, and manage projects efficiently.

- **Document Sharing and Collaboration:** Use Google Docs or Microsoft 365 to create, share, and collaborate on documents in real-time, making team collaboration more efficient.

By integrating these technologies into your daily life, you can enhance productivity, streamline tasks, improve your health and well-being, and stay better connected with others. The key is to identify the tools that best fit your needs and help you accomplish your goals.

You said:
Continuous Learning
ChatGPT said:
ChatGPT
Continuous learning is the process of constantly developing new skills, knowledge, and abilities throughout your life. It's essential for personal growth, professional development, and adapting to the changing world. In a world where industries evolve rapidly and new information is always emerging, fostering a mindset of continuous learning is key to staying competitive, engaged, and fulfilled. Here's how you can embrace and implement continuous learning in your life:

1. Embrace a Growth Mindset

- **Believe in Your Ability to Improve:** Cultivate a mindset that you can always learn and grow, no matter where you are in life. This means accepting challenges, learning from mistakes, and continuously striving to improve.
- **Seek Challenges:** Embrace tasks or subjects that push your boundaries. A growth mindset thrives on overcoming obstacles and expanding knowledge.
- **Learn from Failure:** See mistakes as opportunities to learn. Analyzing what went wrong can lead to improved strategies and better outcomes next time.

2. Use Online Learning Platforms

- Enroll in Online Courses: Platforms like Coursera, edX, Udemy, and LinkedIn Learning offer courses on a variety of topics, from coding and marketing to personal development and leadership. You can learn at your own pace and gain skills that are relevant to your interests or career goals.
- Specialization Programs: Some platforms offer certifications and specialization programs that provide in-depth knowledge of specific areas, such as digital marketing, data analysis, or business management.
- Webinars and Workshops: Attend live or recorded webinars on topics of interest. These often provide current, relevant, and expert insights.

3. Read Regularly

- Books: Commit to reading books regularly. Explore both non-fiction (on subjects such as personal growth, history, technology, or self-help) and fiction (for creativity and broadening your perspective).
- Podcasts and Audiobooks: If you have a busy lifestyle, consider listening to podcasts or audiobooks during commutes, workouts, or chores. Platforms like Audible, Spotify, or Apple Podcasts offer a wide selection.
- Articles and Journals: Stay updated by reading relevant articles, journals, or industry reports. Websites like Medium, Harvard Business Review, or Google Scholar can help you stay informed.

4. Engage in Microlearning

- Short Learning Sessions: Microlearning involves consuming small, digestible chunks of information. This could be in the form of short articles, podcasts, videos, or app-based learning modules.
- Daily Learning Goals: Dedicate just 15-30 minutes per day to learning something new, whether it's a quick tutorial on YouTube, a brief article, or a podcast. Over time, these small efforts add up.

5. Join Communities and Networks

- Professional Groups: Join industry-specific groups, forums, or online communities like Reddit, Quora, or Slack communities. Engaging with people

who share similar interests can help you stay updated on new trends and innovations.
- Social Learning: Collaborate with others in your learning journey. Share what you know, ask questions, and discuss new ideas. Learning from peers can provide different perspectives and deepen your understanding.
- Mentorship: Find a mentor or coach who can guide your learning path, offering advice, resources, and feedback. Alternatively, mentoring someone else can also be a powerful way to reinforce your own learning.

6. Develop New Skills

- Cross-Disciplinary Learning: Expand your learning beyond your usual areas of expertise. For example, if you're a writer, learning about graphic design or coding can open up new creative and career possibilities.
- Hands-On Practice: Experiment with what you learn by putting it into practice. Whether it's coding, writing, or public speaking, hands-on experience reinforces new concepts and makes them easier to internalize.
- Try New Tools and Technology: Keep exploring new software, apps, and technologies related to your field. Learning how to use tools like Excel, Photoshop, Trello, or Python can boost your capabilities.

7. Attend Conferences and Industry Events

- Stay Current: Conferences, seminars, and workshops are great opportunities to learn about the latest trends in your field, network with professionals, and get insights from experts.
- Virtual Events: If you can't attend in person, consider virtual conferences and webinars. They often offer the same valuable content but with the added benefit of convenience and flexibility.

8. Keep a Learning Journal

- Document Your Progress: Keep track of the new things you learn, what challenges you faced, and how you overcame them. Reflecting on your journey

will help you identify patterns in your learning process and areas where you can improve.
- Set Learning Goals: Regularly set short-term and long-term learning goals. These can be specific (e.g., "Learn Python basics") or general (e.g., "Read one book a month").
- Review and Reflect: Periodically review your journal or notes to evaluate how much progress you've made, which goals you've achieved, and where you still need to focus.

9. Utilize Social Media for Learning

- Follow Experts and Thought Leaders: Social media platforms like Twitter, LinkedIn, and Instagram are great places to follow industry leaders, experts, and innovators. Many share valuable content that can help you stay informed and inspired.
- Learning Hashtags and Groups: Look for learning hashtags (#learn, #growthmindset, #continuouslearning) or specialized groups on platforms like Reddit and Facebook for curated content and discussions.

10. Experiment with New Learning Methods

- Gamified Learning: Apps like Duolingo (for languages), Khan Academy (for various subjects), or Skillshare offer gamified learning experiences that make acquiring knowledge more fun and engaging.
- Interactive Learning: Engage in platforms like Codecademy or LeetCode, which allow you to learn through interactive coding exercises or problem-solving.
- Project-Based Learning: Work on real-world projects that require the application of your learning. For example, if you're learning coding, create a website or app. If you're learning design, try building a portfolio.

11. Set a Learning Routine

- Consistency Over Intensity: Establish a routine that allows for steady, consistent learning, even if it's just 20-30 minutes per day. Consistency is key to retaining information and making learning a lifelong habit.

- **Morning or Evening Sessions:** Allocate specific times in the day for focused learning. Many find that learning in the morning or before bed is more productive because the brain is more alert or relaxed.

12. Teach What You Learn

- **Reinforce Learning by Teaching:** One of the best ways to truly understand a concept is by teaching it to someone else. Start a blog, make tutorial videos, or explain topics to peers. Teaching helps solidify your knowledge and build confidence.
- **Create Learning Content:** Create your own notes, presentations, or even write articles about what you've learned. This not only reinforces your understanding but also helps others in their learning journeys.

13. Stay Curious

- **Ask Questions:** Curiosity is at the heart of continuous learning. Always ask "why" and "how" to deepen your understanding of the world around you.
- **Explore New Interests:** Try learning something outside of your comfort zone—whether it's a new language, a new software tool, or a creative hobby. Expanding your horizons can lead to unexpected learning opportunities and personal growth.

By integrating continuous learning into your routine, you foster personal growth, increase your adaptability, and open yourself up to new opportunities in both your personal and professional life. It's not about mastering everything but rather embracing the journey of lifelong learning.

www.ingramcontent.com/pod-product-compliance
Lightning Source LLC
Chambersburg PA
CBHW051940210526
45473CB00006B/2320